Anonymous

Tithes Ordinary and Extraordinary

How to deal with them

Anonymous

Tithes Ordinary and Extraordinary
How to deal with them

ISBN/EAN: 9783337037215

Printed in Europe, USA, Canada, Australia, Japan

Cover: Foto ©Suzi / pixelio.de

More available books at **www.hansebooks.com**

TITHES ORDINARY AND

EXTRAORDINARY:

HOW TO DEAL WITH THEM.

THE "MARK LANE EXPRESS"

Prize Essays.

LONDON:

THE AGRICULTURAL PRESS COMPANY, Limited,

Clement's House, Clement's Inn Passage, W.C.

TITHES ORDINARY AND EXTRAORDINARY:

HOW TO DEAL WITH THEM.

By WILLIAM WATT, Aberdeen.

THE Tithe Question of the present day turns almost exclusively upon the Commutation Act of 1836. This Act brought substantial relief from a long-standing grievance and injustice. More than one-half of the tithable property of the country had been the creation of modern times. Whenever a piece of waste land was reclaimed and cropped the tithe-owner stepped in to claim his share of the produce—reaping where he had not sown, and gathering where he had not strawed. The old tithe system with its anomalies was borne with for a long time, but at last the patience of English farmers became exhausted, and to remedy what was at the time the most pressing of their grievances the Commutation Act was passed. It was not a perfect remedy, but the result of a compromise, and vitiated by certain radical defects. The agricultural interest, however, accepted it as a boon, and such in truth it was ; but as time went on the defects became more and more apparent, and new evils began to be experienced under its operation.

Before Commutation, tithes, though an annoyance to the farmer, were in their ultimate incidence a tax on the consumer. By the Act of 1836 they became a rent-charge ; whether paid by landlord or tenant in the first instance, they became, theoretically at least, a deduction from rent. How were they a tax on the consumer ? it may be asked. A general answer will suffice for the present purpose. The Corn Laws kept the price of grain at a high level, and limited the supply from abroad. One-tenth of the gross produce of the land went to the tithe-owner—under which designation I include throughout this paper the lay impropriator. A tenth of the gross produce was obviously much more than a tenth of the farmer's net income, the other nine-tenths having to bear rent, taxes, and all the costs of production. It was also obviously much more than a tenth of the rent. Generally speaking it may have been about a fifth, or in the ratio of 20 per cent. to what the landlord received as the hire of average land. The tithe was almost entirely net income, and formed a very heavy burden on the agricultural interest. On inferior lands, the produce of which was just sufficient to bear the cost of cultivation, it took precedence of the landlord's rent. Land could not be kept in cultivation, indeed, unless nine-tenths of the produce were sufficient to pay the farmer's costs, leaving one-tenth for the tithe-owner, and nothing for the landlord ; and on these terms the interest of the landlord was against corn-growing. The land was to him more profitable as sheep walk or rabbit-warren, when, but for the tithe, it would have yielded crops with a margin of profit and rent. Independently, therefore, of the peculiarly obnoxious manner in which it was levied, the tithe impeded and hampered agricultural enterprise. When relief came an important change was at once apparent. Whether land fell out of cultivation or additional land was brought under tillage, the rent charge was now an immovable quantity. Under these altered conditions not a little thin and infertile land began to be rapidly reclaimed from the waste. One of the law-made impediments to the production of food having been removed, an additional acreage was immediately ploughed, sown, and reaped; and thus a tangible benefit accrued to the general community in those Corn Law times from the Tithe Commutation Act of 1836.

The gain to the farmer was more doubtful. Too often he was tempted to offer excessive rent for the lands which the commutation of tithes made him desirous to cultivate, and no very long time elapsed before the repeal of the Corn Laws introduced new conditions little to his advantage. Bad seasons told severely upon the farmers of the inferior lands. The imperfections of the Act itself also soon became painfully apparent. The work of valuation for the rent-charge proceeded slowly. Still slowlier went on that redemption of the tithes which the Act permitted. If the rent-charge had become theoretically a claim against the landlord the Act failed to prevent him from passing it on to the tenant. The farmer paying tithe rent-charge pays so much less rent, it may be said. But this is a meagre and inaccurate statement of his position. He is always at the mercy of the seasons. Storms and floods at certain periods of the year may involve him in incalculable loss. His crops and his live stock are subject to the ravages of blight and disease. In bad seasons and periods of misfortune in the days preceding Commutation, he had less tithe taken from him than in good seasons. The tithe was proportioned to the ¦bounty of nature. It rose in years of abundance and fell in years of scarcity. But now-a-days the payment substituted for tithes is apt to be highest when the produce is least. The seven years' average of corn prices, upon which the rent charge is based, if it serves to moderate the fluctuations in the amount of this payment, serves also to render it unduly onerous in seasons of adversity and failure. The most disastrous year of recent times has just been passed through, and for that year the rent-charge was far above its average of the last forty years, and still farther above the amount that was deemed an equitable satisfaction of the tithe-owner's claims when the Commutation Act was passed. Since 1836 the fluctuations in the amount of the rent-charge have been very considerable indeed. The quantities of corn assigned to the tithe-owner in that year as the equivalent of £100 in money yielded him only about £90 twenty years later. During the last twenty-two years, however—half the period that has elapsed since Commutation—the rent-charge has only thrice been below the par of 1836, and by but a trifling percentage in the three exceptional years. The average of the twenty-two years has been £106 18s. 8d., or nearly 7 per cent. above the original fixture. For last year, when the harvest was one of the worst on record—certainly the worst by far that has been experienced since tithes were commuted —the value of the rent-charge was £109 17s. 9d. For 1878 it was £112 7s. 5¼d., for 1874 about the same amount, for 1875 higher, and never below £108 since 1871. Since 1871 only two harvests have yielded an average return, and five have fallen far short of the average,—at least as the average used to be estimated, for it is becoming a serious question whether the standard of yield will not have to be revised. Deficient harvests and high rent-charge have thus gone together. Year after year the farmer has been kept on the rack, unable, too often, to prevent his capital from being eaten away ; and all the while he has been harassed by exceptionally high exactions to meet the claims of the tithe-owner. With the rent-charge two shillings or more in the pound above the Commutation fixture, crops deficient, and prices low—it is a fine time for the tithe-owner, anything but a fine time for the tithe-paying farmer !

The main scope and purpose of the arrangement of 1836,

was to commute the variable tithe into a corn-rent payable in money. The corn forming the corn-rent was to be a fixed quantity, and permanently apportioned to the lands of each parish by Commissioners appointed under the Act. The tithe-owner was thus to receive every year the money equivalent of a fixed and definite number of quarters of corn. This corn was to consist of wheat, barley, and oats— not equal quantities, nor in proportion to acreage or yield, but the quantities constituting equal values according to the official average prices of the seven years immediately preceding 1836. By this scale the proportions for £100 of rent-charge were 94·95 bushels of wheat, 168·42 of barley, and 242·42 of oats, each of these quantities representing the value of £33 6s. 8d. Such were the proportions fixed in the Act for all time coming, and upon which every payment of rent-charge was to be made. Whether only one species of grain, or two species, or three, or none at all, were grown on the land thenceforward mattered not. The rent-charge had to be paid on the triplex scale, its amount being for each year the mean of the previous seven years' official average prices applied to these respective proportions. The prices on which the proportions were determined were for wheat, 56s. 2d. per quarter; for barley, 31s. 6d.; and for oats, 22s.

These facts involve some of the leading points at which readjustment is required.

First, as to the composition of the rent-charge. The high proportions assigned to barley and oats give those grains a preponderating influence on the result. A rise or fall of a shilling per quarter in the mean septennial average of wheat affects the rent-charge only to the extent of about twelve shillings per £100. A similar rise or fall on barley makes twenty-one shillings and on oats thirty shillings of difference. The order of importance of the three grains in English agriculture is thus reversed in the rent-charge arrangement. But this is not all. Wheat, to which so very subordinate a place is assigned, has averaged, since Commutation, about 2s. 10d. per quarter below the par value adopted in 1836. Barley, on the contrary, has averaged for the forty-four years 2s. 8d., and oats 1s. 3d. above the original fixtures. Thus it has come about that while the staple grain has fallen in price, the corn-rent in lieu of tithe has been about two and three-quarters per cent. above the Commutation level on the average of the subsequent period; and, as we have seen, the disparity has been much greater during the latter half of the time. I think it will be generally allowed, on consideration of these facts, that equity requires that the tripartite arrangement should be reconsidered. Joseph Hume's proposal of half-wheat and quarter each barley and oats would be better ; and fixed money rent-charge best.

Secondly, as to the mode of striking the averages. The 150 selected markets from which official returns are made are not the best possible selection, regard being had to the course of the corn trade in these modern days. Many important markets are omitted : not a few unimportant are included. This, however, is a matter of detail, not of itself, perhaps, very vital. But the returns from the markets in the list are often most imperfect. The West Riding Chamber of Agriculture not very long ago made public the fact that of all the dealers attending the important market of Wakefield not one had for six weeks on end made the returns to the corn inspector that are required by law. Throughout the country great laxity and remissness notoriously prevail in regard to these returns. But even when they are duly made they are not just to the grower or to the payer of the rent-charge whether he is the grower or not. They are returns of prices *in the market*, and include costs of carriage and profits of dealers and intermediaries. They are not growers' prices. They make no allowance for the " tail-corn " consumed on the farm, or for the inferior samples increasingly used in these days for feeding purposes instead of being sent to market. They are the prices of the choicest portion of the crop, and not of the crop as a whole. The averages based on them must therefore be fallacious, unduly favourable to the tithe-owner, unjust to the payer of tithe be he farmer or landlord, doubly unjust to the farmer in so far as they serve to aggravate a burden not properly his. Here again a fixed money rent-charge would save all heart-burning and sense of wrong.

Thirdly, as to the septennial average. This also is open to question, and chiefly because of its tendency, already referred to, to maintain the rent-charge at a high level through periods of agricultural depression.

In considering how the rent-charge should be dealt with so as to remove the anomalies and grievances connected with it, some not unimportant hints may be derived from the settlement of the tithe question effected long ago in Scotland. The Scotch landlords, at their county meetings, have lately been complaining a little of the growing disposition of the presbyteries to exact the uttermost farthing allowed by that settlement, and are taking counsel together at Edinburgh on this and other matters concerning their relations with the Kirk. But the farmer has been completely emancipated. Questions about teinds (as tithes are called in Scotland) are no affair of his. He is free to pursue his own business, and is an entirely disinterested spectator of the disputes between presbyteries and heritors. After the Reformation the people of Scotland became restive under the teinds, which were an oppressive deduction from the scanty produce of the land, and obnoxious from the way in which they were collected. In the course of the 17th century the Scotch Parliament appointed several executive commissions to deal with ecclesiastical matters, and some at least of these commissions were invested with powers to value, sell, and otherwise dispose of the teinds. At the union with England the powers of the last of these commissions were transferred to a newly constituted "Court of Teinds," presided over by the judges of the Court of Session. Questions concerning the temporalities of the Church are still dealt with by the Court of Teinds. From the time it was instituted the landowners were enabled to obtain through its instrumentality a judicial valuation of the tithes. A fifth of the rent at the date of the valuation was regarded as the whole tithe, and the Court of Teinds was empowered to grant such proportion of this fifth as it might see fit, to form the stipend of the minister. The remainder called the free or unappropriated teinds, was left in the possession of the landowner. As long as any part of the teinds remained thus unappropriated to ecclesiastical use the minister was entitled to apply once every twenty years for an augmentation of stipend. In many parishes the teinds are now exhausted, but in many others there is still a balance left. The application for an increase of stipend, having been sanctioned by the Presbytery, goes to the Court of Teinds. The landowners may oppose. The Court decides the case on its merits, and apportions such increase as it may grant upon the lands of the parish according to the free teinds for which each is liable. The Scotch like the English tithe has been commuted into a corn rent payable in money ; but there is an essential difference between the modes in which the amount to be paid is determined. In Scotland the standard by which the payments are ruled is not a compound septennial average, but the fiars' prices of the year. These prices are struck for each county annually. The practice differs a little in different counties, but the system, briefly described, is this :—A Fiars' Court is held in the spring, presided over by the Sheriff of the county, and to which a jury of landowners, farmers, corn-dealers, accountants, and other respectable persons is summoned. Witnesses — principal growers and principal buyers — are likewise summoned from all districts of the county, and are required to bring with them schedules setting forth the quantities and prices involved in the actual transactions in which they have been concerned. Cognisance is taken only of first transactions, and grain is classified into first and second quality.

The advantages of this system over the English are :— (1) That it gives a growers' and not a dealers' average ; (2) that it adapts itself to local circumstances, and, in particular, to local prices ; (3) that it lets every year bear its own burdens, the money value of the teinds rising and falling with prices ; (4) that a distinction is made between first and second quality of corn ; and (5) that the evidence is full and trustworthy, and the prices struck by a jury consisting of men of good standing, under the direction of a trained lawyer having daily practise in the exercise of judicial functions. As I have said, the tithes are in Scotland purely a landlords' question; and the settlement on this basis has worked very well. Without much difficulty the system might be adapted to English circumstances. Witnesses might be called, as in Scotland, to give evidence before a court and jury, which might be presided over by the Chairman of Quarter Sessions. Alternatively there is the County Court Judge, to whose jurisdiction the matter might be assigned if it were thought that quarter sessions are too intimately connected with landlords' interests to be a sufficiently impartial tribunal. In either case there would be the safeguard of a jury and of publicity. If the corn-rent-charge is to be maintained, it is obviously right that the price to the grower should be taken as the foundation of the averages. A separate determination of prices for each county would also be a great improvement. The smallest reform worth the name would be to multiply the number of the returning markets, and compel the grower to make returns under penalties. But without judicial authority there will never be an efficiently working system.

The substitution for the existing corn-rent of a fixed money rent-charge, payable by the landlord, would put an end to difficulties, and save much time and trouble. This is the true and simple solution of the tithe problem. The adjustment of the new commutation, with due regard to the interests involved, would be a work of some little delicacy, perhaps ; but Parliament, after full discussion of the subject, would doubtless come to a decision not out of harmony with common sense and equity. The average cash value of the rent-charge since 1836, would probably commend itself to many impartial minds as a leading point to be considered in formulating such a re-arrangement.

The important question of redemption would thus be in some degree simplified. The value of the rent-charge would be easy to calculate ; and as the security would be of the highest order, the purchase-money would be obtainable on moderate terms, either with or without the intervention of the Government. It could be repaid by instalments over a series of years. In the case of the tithes devoted to ecclesiastical use, some three-fourths of the whole, the redemption-money would be vested in the nation ; the annuity derivable from it taking the place of the rent-charge in furnishing the incomes of the clergy. The Act of 1836 provided for redemption on the agreement of the owners of two-thirds in value of the lands and tithes respectively, such agreement being confirmed by the Tithe Commissioners. Progress has not, however, been rapid ; and it would, doubtless, be accelerated, or at least there would be less temptation to hold out against it, were the rent-charge absolutely fixed and no fluctuation either way in prospect.

It may be demurred that a rigid money-rent would be unfair to the tithe owner—that the settlement of 1836 has yielded him a considerable increment on the average of years, and that a hard and fast money standard would bo less to his advantage. To this it may be answered that there is no assurance that barley and oats will continue to rise in price. It is quite possible that instead of rising they may fall, and on the whole the average of the forty-four years seems a liberal proposal to make for the further commutation which the general interest renders expedient. The tithe-owner has contributed nothing to the agricultural value of the land on which he holds a preferential dividend-claim. His preference dividend is very commonly equal to a fourth or even a third of the landlord's rent. To cite only one instance, one that is already public property, Mr. Mechi recently mentioned the case of a farm in Essex, on which the tithe came to seven shillings an acre, while the landlord's rent had fallen far below that amount, whereas in better times the same land had been rented at upwards of a pound an acre. It seems perfectly fair and just to treat the tithe rent-charge as a preference dividend, not liable to fluctuation, and subject to redemption at a fair actuarial value.

Thus far I have been considering only the ordinary tithes and the best mode of dealing with them. The "extra-ordinary" tithes introduce a new set of considerations. Amongst their other duties, the Tithe Commissioners were to form the lands in any parish in which there were hop-gardens, market-gardens, or orchards, into a "district" within which the tithe rent-charge was to be divided into two parts—ordinary and extraordinary. The ordinary was to apply to all lands cultivated under the usual rotations; the extraordinary to be an additional burden on the market-gardens, hop-grounds, and orchards, ceasing in the event of the lands ceasing to be thus employed. When fresh lands come to be cultivated for the first time as market or hop-gardens, after the passing of the Commutation Act, they were to be rated with an additional rent-charge, so as to bring up their total liability to the amount of the extraordinary rent-charge per acre in the district. Here was a new tax upon industry operating as a serious discouragement to the improved cultivation of the soil ; and its evils were indefinitely extended by an Amending Act, passed twenty years ago, by which the Commissioners were empowered, upon the application of interested parties, to declare the lands in any parish of England and Wales a district within which an extraordinary rent-charge may be fixed by them if any portion of the parish has been cultivated as hop-gardens or market-gardens since the passing of the Act of 1836. The door was thus opened for a great deal of litigation. Agricultural and market-garden produce shade into each other by fine gradations. Potatoes, cabbages, beet, and even peas and beans, are garden as well as field crops. In parts of the centre and north-east of Scotland, the strawberry is a field crop. Extraordinary tithe was, in point of fact, demanded, in respect of certain land in Cornwall newly reclaimed and planted with potatoes ; and exemption was not secured until a special Act of Parliament was passed for the purpose in 1873. Cornwall, however, is exceptionally favoured ; and extraordinary rent-charge at rates varying from 6s. to 24s. an acre or upwards, is levied on much of the land in several counties of the south and west of England. In its practical effect the extraordinary rent-charge is virtually a tax on specific articles. Of the products—hops, fruit, and vegetables—subject to this indirect tax there are yearly importations to the value of five or six millions. To that extent does the foreigner compete successfully in the English markets with the overtaxed English producers. The extraordinary rent-charge acts as a bounty on importation, and discourages improvement. The farmer brings additional produce out of the land by cultivating and cropping it on market gardening principles, and no sooner does he begin to reap his reward than the tithe-owner, who has contributed nothing to the result, steps in to demand his share of the produce. Within less than an hour's railway journey of London, there is much uncultivated land that will some day be turned to better account. It would probably be so at once but for the extraordinary tithe that weighs so heavily on the inferior soils to which it is applied. The Metropolis and other great towns are but indifferently furnished with fresh fruit and vegetables, although the home supply is largely supplemented from France and Belgium. With a better supply the demand would increase, and there will be increasing scope for the development of this branch of rural economy. Meanwhile the extraordinary tithe operates seriously to its prejudice. Alike in the interests of the producer and of the general community as consumers, it is imperative that this obnoxious impost should be got rid of.

The first thing to be done with the extraordinary tithe is to pass an Act to prevent its extension to lands at present free. Mr. Inderwick, the member for Rye, is moving in the matter, and has in hand a bill having this for its object. Further, there is the question of redemption. I have spoken of the ordinary tithe rent-charge as a preferential dividend from the land. In like manner the extraordinary tithe may be compared to a terminable and uncertain annuity. It may cease at any time through a change in the mode of culture. Should Mr. Inderwick be successful in his endeavour to prevent the imposition of the tax on land not now subject to it he will have done more to provide a remedy for the existing evil than will be apparent from the terms of his bill. Free land would soon come into competition with land that is burdened. The burdened land would be less in demand, and in process of time the extraordinary tithe might be expected to die a natural death. In place of waiting for this it would probably be found worth while for landlords to pay and tithe-owners to accept a few years' purchase as the price of immediate redemption. What the purchase value should be I cannot profess to determine. Obviously for an uncertain security like the extraordinary tithe it would be very much less than for the ordinary rent-charge. Seven years' purchase was thought an equitable allowance for the extraordinary tithe in 1836, and it will hardly be maintained that its value has been enhanced since then.

The whole subject of tithes is of not a little practical interest to the agriculturist. By being subjected, as he too often is, to the burden of the ordinary rent-charge, he is made to suffer vicariously in times of adversity when otherwise he has more than enough to bear. The ordinary rent-charge is distinctly a charge on the land. The extraordinary rent-charge, on the other hand, is a tax on production and an impediment to the cultivation of the soil. The one should be changed into a fixed money rent, subject to redemption, and payable directly by the landlord; the other should be restricted to its present area in the first instance, and then redeemed where practicable, or, failing that, allowed to disappear by a gradual process of decay.

SECOND PRIZE ESSAY.

By ALBERT BATH, Colgates Farm, Sevenoaks, Kent.

Part I.—ORDINARY TITHES.

As the payment of tithes is now agitating the minds of agriculturists and others, I consider it a very seasonable time to elicit what facts we can concerning them.   The question arises in the minds of many thoughtful men whether, in the face of heavy foreign competition and free trade (which is a blessing to the million), the imposition of tithes for the support of the richest church in Christendom is compatible with the present altered times; and if tithes should still be exacted from the producer of food, whether it would not be to the benefit and prosperity of our country that they should be used for educational purposes and for the easement of local burdens.

It is universally admitted that the payment of tithes was, in its commencement, free and spontaneous; and although it was afterwards enjoined as a religious duty, yet, until the establishment of the parochial right, every one was at liberty to give his tithes to any religious or ecclesiastical persons at his discretion.   A rector could no more demand tithes of any of the lands within his parish without showing a particular title by grant or prescription than he could demand inheritance of the lands themselves.   The first written mention of tithes in any English law that I can find was in the year 786, when a synod was held wherein the payment of tithes was strongly enjoined. The laity were not at first bound by this canon until it was confirmed by two kingdoms of the Heptarchy (Mercia and Northumberland), by a Parliament of the bishops, dukes, senators, and people. Later on I notice that in 844 King Ethelwolf, at an assembly held at Winchester, granted a tenth of all his lands, free from all taxes and impositions of every kind. Tithes were of three kinds; prædial tithes, arising only either of the fruits of the ground, as corn, hay, hemp, or the fruits of the orchards, as apples, plums, pears, &c. ; secondly, personal tithes, arising out of the industry and labour of men, either by handicraft or buying, selling, &c. ; and thirdly, mixed tithes, arising partly out of the ground, and partly of the industry of men, as lands, pigs, calves, cheese, and milk. I next find that Athelstan in 928, at a great Council, made the following canon :—"I, King Athelstan, by the advice of Wolfstein, my archbishop, and my other bishops, strictly charge you all, my reeves in all parts of my kingdom, in the name of God and the saints, and as you value my favour, to pay tithes, both of cattle and corn, on all my lands, and I further ordain that all my bishops aldermen shall pay the tithes of their lands, and they shall give it in charge to all who are under their jurisdiction to do the same. All this I command to be carried into execution by the time appointed." Then in 958, a canon of King Edgar, wherein the clergy are recommended to earnestly exhort the people to pay their dues to the Church at the proper time—"their plough alm fifteen nights after Easter, their tithes of young animals at Pentecost, their tithes of corn at All Saints, their Peter's pence at Lammas, their church scot at Martinmas." In the reign of King Canute, among the canons I find penalties threatened for failing to pay tithe of corn, cattle, church scot,

Rome scot, plough alms, light scot, and soul scot. In the beginning of the reign of King John, about the year 1200, all tithes of lands which were not then vested in any ecclesiastical person or body were annexed by the general law of the land to the rector of the parish in which such lands were situate. For this reason the right of a rector to all the tithes arising within his parish, is usually termed by lawyers his common law right ; and this right is perfectly distinct from those particular interests in tithes which were created by the arbitrary grants or consecrations of private persons before the establishment of the parochial and common law right, and which are now denominated portions of tithes. For these portions were never annexed to any rectory, nor do they, either in point of fact or in contemplation of law, belong, or bear any relation to, the rectories of the parishes in which they are situate, but are wholly collateral to the inheritance of the rectory. Nor can they be legally united to the rectory ; for if a portion of tithes and the rectory should happen to be vested in the same person for an equal estate in fee, the portion will not merge in the rectory, but will continue a distinct inheritance.

Coming down to the time of King Edward III., I find he passed a law that barren lands and woods of more than twenty years' growth should be exempt from tithes, and this he did without consulting the Church. I will now mention the Reformation. This was effected by King Henry VIII., who became displeased and discontented with the Pope because he would not grant him a divorce from his Queen, in order that he might marry her maid of honour, Anne Boleyn ; renounced the Pope's supremacy (though himself a Papist), and assumed it himself ; and by Act of a Parliament which he awed into submission, got the tithes and other ecclesiastical property transferred from their original holders to the clergy of the new Church. When Queen Mary, in her devotion to Rome, and Elizabeth, in her aspiration after spiritual supremacy, sought to make similar changes, they had only to command their Parliaments and the work was done. The chorus of the song called " The Vicar of Bray," viz. :—

> " And this is law, I will maintain
> Until my dying day, sir—
> Whatsoever king may reign,
> Still I'll be Vicar of Bray, sir,"

brings to our minds the many changes that the country underwent as regards the State religion ; and the Vicar of Bray, to prevent losing his tithes and position, was not scrupulous in changing his religion from Roman Catholicism to Protestantism, and *vice versâ*, from time to time as the monarchs at their pleasure brought about the alteration.

From what I have stated, it is shown with perfect clearness that tithes owed their existence not to any pious bequest, but simply to the creation of law. At first they were a voluntary offering ; but after a time, people failing to pay, the civil power stepped in and converted them into a national tax, and an increasing one, as it is estimated that more than two-thirds of the present tithable property of the Church has arisen during the last three hundred years, from the cultivation of waste lands formerly belonging to the Crown, or, in other words, to the people. Seven years after cultivation, these lands became subject to tithes.

As I have previously stated, tithes owe their existence to the creation of law, and this is proved by Parliament legislating upon them far differently than it does on our private property. A later proof is the Tithe Commutation Act, 1836. This Act altered the mode of assessing and collecting the annual value, but did not in any way affect the tenure of this kind of property. The ownership and the conditions of use remain precisely what they were before the Act was passed. The adoption of the term " rent-charge," however, in lieu of " tithes," has very materially contributed to the spread of the notion that the payments with which individuals are in the habit of voluntarily charging their landed estates, as a provision for different branches of their families, or in compensation for some services performed, and the payments which are now annually made to beneficed clergymen under that name, are analogous. I will give some sections of the above Act, as they may be of interest. Being a tenant-farmer and not a lawyer, I shall not presume to interpret their meaning, but merely make a few comments on some of the clauses that most affect agriculturists. As a kind of introduction to the Act I will give the first section :—

Anno Sexto et Septimo
Gulielmi IV., Regis.
Cap. LXXI.
An Act for the Commutation of Tithes in England and Wales.
[13th August, 1836.]

Whereas it is expedient to amend the laws relating to tithes in England and Wales, and to provide the means for an adequate compensation for tithes, and for the commutation thereof. Be it therefore enacted by the King's most excellent Majesty, by and with the advice and consent of the Lords Spiritual and Temporal, and Commons, in this present Parliament assembled, and by the authority of the same, that it shall be lawful for one of his Majesty's principal Secretaries of State to appoint two fit persons to be Commissioners to carry this Act into execution, and for the Archbishop of Canterbury, under his hand and archiepiscopal seal, to appoint one fit person to be a Commissioner to carry this Act into execution, and for the said Archbishop and Secretary of State, at their joint pleasure, to remove any one or more of the Commissioners so appointed ; and upon every vacancy in the office of Commissioner some other fit person shall be appointed to the said office in the same manner and by the same authority as the Commissioner whose vacancy is thereby supplied ; and until such appointment it shall be lawful for the continuing Commissioners or Commissioner to act as if no vacancy had occurred.

22. And be it enacted, That at the said meeting, or at some adjournment thereof, or at some other parochial meeting to be called in like manner, either before or after the confirmation of the agreement, the owners of lands subject to tithes in the said parish, or their agents, present at the meeting, may appoint a valuer or valuers ; and in case the majority in respect of number and the majority in respect to interest shall not agree upon the appointment, then they shall appoint two or such other even number of valuers as shall be then agreed on by such landowners, half of such number to be chosen by a majority in respect of number, and the other half by a majority in respect of interest, of such landowners then present.

33. And be it enacted, That as soon as may be after the choosing of such valuer or valuers, and after the confirmation of the said agreement, the valuer or valuers so chosen shall apportion the total sum agreed to be paid by way of rent-charge instead of tithes, and the expenses of the appointment, amongst the several lands in the said parish, according to such principles of apportionment as shall be agreed upon at the meeting at which the valuer or valuers shall be chosen, or if no principles shall be then agreed upon for the guidance of the valuer or valuers, then, having regard to the average titheable produce and productive quality of the lands, according to his or their discretion and judgment, but subject in each case to the provisions hereinafter contained, and so that in each case the several lands shall have the full benefit of every modus and composition real, prescriptive and customary payment, and of every exemption from or non-liability to tithes relating to the said lands respectively, and having regard to the several tithes to which the said lands are severally liable ; provided that it shall be lawful for the said valuers when an even number is chosen, by any writing under their hands, to appoint an umpire before they proceed upon the business of such apportionment, and the decision of the umpire on the questions in difference between the valuers shall be binding on them, and shall be adopted by them in apportionment.

37. And be it enacted, That in every case in which the commissioners shall intend making such award, notice thereof shall be given in such manner as to them shall seem fit ; and

after the expiration of twenty-one days after such notice shall have been given, the commissioners or some assistant commissioner shall, except in the cases for which provision is hereinafter made, proceed to ascertain the clear average value (after making all just deductions on account of the expense of collecting, preparing for sale, and marketing where such tithes have been taken in kind), of the tithes in the said parish, according to the average of seven years, preceding Christmas in the year one thousand eight hundred and thirty-five; provided that if during the said period of seven years, or any part thereof, the said tithes or any part thereof shall be compounded for or demised to the owner or occupier of any of the said lands in consideration of any rent or payment instead of tithes; the amount of such composition or rent or sum agreed to be paid instead of tithes shall be taken as the clear value of the tithes included in such composition, demise, or agreement during the time for which the same shall have been made; and the commissioners or assistant commissioner shall award the average annual value of the said seven years so ascertained as the sum to be taken for calculating the rent-charge to be paid as a permanent commutation of the said tithes; provided also, that whenever it shall appear to the commissioners that the party entitled to any such rent or composition shall in any one or more of the said seven years have allowed any abatement from the amount of such rent or composition on the ground of the same having in such year or years been higher than the sum fairly payable, by way of compensation for the tithe, but not otherwise, then and in every such case such diminished amount, after making such abatement as aforesaid, shall be deemed and taken to have been the sum agreed to be paid for any such year or years; provided also, that in estimating the value of the said tithes the commissioners or assistant commissioner shall estimate the same without making any deduction therefrom on account of any parliamentary, parochial, county, and other rates, charges, and assessments, to which the said tithes are liable; and whenever the said tithes shall have been demised or compounded for on the principle of the rent or composition being paid free from all such rates, charges, and assessments, or any part thereof, the said commissioners or assistant commissioner shall have regard to that circumstance, and shall make such an addition on account thereof as shall be equivalent.

42. And be it enacted, That the amount which shall be charged by any such apportionment as hereinafter provided upon any hop grounds or market gardens in any district so to be assigned shall be distinguished into two parts, which shall be called the ordinary charge and the extraordinary charge, and the extraordinary charge shall be a rate per imperial acre, and so in proportion for less quantities of ground, according to the discretion of the valuers or commissioners or assistant commissioner by whom the apportionment shall be made as aforesaid ; and all lands whereof the tithes shall have been commuted under this Act, and which shall cease to be cultivated as hop grounds or market gardens at any time after such commutation, shall be charged after the Thirty-first day of December next following such change of cultivation only with the ordinary charge upon such lands ; and all lands in any such district the tithes whereof shall have been commuted under this Act, and which shall be newly cultivated as hop grounds or market gardens at any time after such commutation, shall be charged with an additional amount of rent-charge per imperial acre, equal to the extraordinary charge per acre upon hop grounds or market gardens respectively in that district ; Provided always, that no such additional amount shall be charged or payable during the first year, and half only of such additional amount during the second year, of such new cultivation ; and an additional rent-charge by way of extraordinary charge upon hop grounds and market gardens, newly cultivated as such beyond the limits of every district in which any extraordinary charge for hop grounds or market gardens respectively shall have been distinguished as aforesaid at the time of the commutation, shall be charged by the commissioners at the time of such new cultivation, upon the request of any person interested therein, if such new cultivation shall have taken place during the continuance of the commission of the said commissioners, and after the expiration of the commission shall be charged in such manner and by such authority as Parliament shall direct, and shall be payable and recoverable in like manner and subject to the same incidents in all respects as an extra-

ordinary charge charged upon any hop grounds or market gardens at the time of commutation.

81. And be it enacted, That in case the said rent-charge shall at any time be in arrear and unpaid for the space of twenty-one days next after any half-yearly day of payment, it shall be lawful for the person entitled to the same, after having given or left ten days' notice in writing at the usual or last known residence of the tenant in possession, to distrain upon the lands liable to the payment thereof, or on any part thereof, for all arrears of the said rent-charge, and to dispose of the distress when taken, and otherwise to act and demean himself in relation thereto as any landlord may for arrears of rent reserved on a common lease for years ; provided that not more than two years' arrears shall at any time be recoverable by distress.

84. Provided always, and be it enacted, That in all cases in which it shall be necessary to make any distress under this Act in respect of any lands in the possession of any person of the persuasion of the people called Quakers, the same may be made upon the goods, chattels, or effects of such person, whether on the premises or elsewhere, but nevertheless to the same amount only and with the same consequences in all respects as if made on the premises ; and that in all cases of distress under this Act upon persons of that persuasion the goods, chattels, or effects which may be distrained shall be sold without its being necessary to impound or keep the same ; Provided always, that no writ under the provision hereinbefore contained shall be issued for assessing or recovering any rent-charge payable under this Act in respect of any lands in the possession of any person of the persuasion aforesaid, unless the same shall be in arrear and unpaid for the space of forty days next after any half-yearly day of payment, without the person entitled thereto being able to find goods, chattels, or effects either on the premises or elsewhere liable to be distrained as aforesaid sufficient to satisfy the arrears to which such lands are liable, together with the reasonable costs of such distress.

85. And be it enacted, That whenever any rent-charge payable under the provisions of this Act, shall be in arrear, notwithstanding any apportionment which may have been made of any such rent-charge, every part of the land situate

in the parish in which such rent-charge shall so be in arrear, and which shall be occupied by the same person who shall be the occupier of the lands on which such rent-charge so in arrear shall have been charged, whether such land shall be occupied by the person occupying the same as the owner thereof, or as tenant thereof, holding under the same landlord under whom he occupies the land on which such rent-charge so in arrear shall have been charged, shall be liable to be distrained upon or entered upon as aforesaid for the purpose of satisfying any arrears of such rent-charge, whether chargeable on the lands on which such distress is taken or such entry made, or upon any other part of the lands so occupied or holden : Provided always that no land shall be liable to be distrained or entered upon for the purpose of satisfying any such rent-charge charged upon lands which shall have been washed away by the sea, or otherwise destroyed by any natural casualty.

96. And be it enacted, That this Act shall extend only to England and Wales.

97. And be it further enacted, That this Act may be amended, altered, or repealed by any Act or Acts to be passed in this present Session of Parliament.

By Section 32, which I give, it will be seen that although the tenants had hereafter to pay in money instead of in kind, they had little or no voice in the matter, bishops, clergymen, and landlords, choosing valuers, and dictating what the tenant-farmer shall pay, at least for 44 years to come. Landlords having interest in the church, being either owners of livings or having sons or relations in the church, did not scruple at the expense of the tiller of the soil to enrich them. Although I was not in existence at the time, I have been told by several farmers living at the time of the alteration that many valuers chosen were incompetent to carry out the grave work they undertook to accomplish. A perusal of Section 33 will show that there was a considerable amount of mist as to how the apportionment should be made, no defined rule being laid down.

Section 37 shows that the values of tithes were to be
calculated upon the average of seven years preceding Christmas, 1835. As Section 67 is a rather important one in this
Act, I here give it :—

67. And be it enacted, That from the first day of January
next following the confirmation of every such appointment
the lands of the said parish shall be absolutely discharged
from the payment of all tithes, except so far as relates to the
liability of any tenant at rack rent dissenting as hereinafter
provided, and instead thereof there shall be payable thenceforth to the person in that behalf mentioned in the said
apportionment a sum of money equal in value, according to
the prices ascertained by the then next preceding advertisement, to the quantity of wheat, barley, and oats respectively
mentioned therein to be payable instead of the said tithes, in
the nature of a rent-charge issuing out of the lands charged
therewith ; and such yearly sum shall be payable by two
equal half-yearly payments on the first day of July and the
first day of January in every year, the first payment, except
in the case of barren reclaimed lands, as hereinafter provided,
being on the first day of July next after the lands shall have
been discharged from tithes as aforesaid ; and such rent-
charge may be recovered at the suit of the person entitled
thereto, his executors or administrators, by distress and entry
as hereinafter mentioned ; and every first day of January
the sum of money thenceforth payable in respect of such
rent-charge shall vary so as always to consist of the price of
the same number of bushels and decimal parts of a bushel of
wheat, barley, and oats respectively, according to the prices
ascertained by the then next preceding advertisement, and
any person entitled from time to time to any such varied rent-
charge shall have the same powers for enforcing payment
thereof as are herein contained concerning the original rent-
charge ; Provided always that nothing herein contained shall
be taken to render any person whomsoever personally liable
to the payment of any such rent-charge ; Provided always,
that the rent-charge which shall be apportioned upon any
lands in the said parish which during any part of the said
period of seven years preceding Christmas One thousand
eight hundred and thirty-five were exempted from tithes by

reason of having been inclosed under any Act of Parliament, or converted from barren heath or waste ground, shall be payable for the first time on the first day of July or first day of January next following the confirmation of the apportionment which shall be nearest to the time at which tithes were or would have become payable for the first time in respect of the said lands if no commutation thereof had taken place.

Under this section it will be seen that the amount of tithe, as awarded or agreed upon, should be divided into three portions, and that every tithe charge should be deemed to be of the value of such number of imperial bushels, and decimal parts of an imperial bushel, of wheat, barley, and oats, as the same would have purchased at the average price for seven years ending Thursday before Christmas Day, 1835, in case one-third part of each rent-charge had been invested in the purchase of wheat, one-third part thereof in the purchase of barley, and the remaining one-third part in purchase of oats. In conformity with the above, I find that £100, expended in wheat, barley, and oats, would purchase the following quantities, at the average prices for seven years to Christmas, 1835, as fixed in the *London Gazette* of December 9th, 1836 :—

£	s.	D.		£	s.	D.		Imp. Bush.
⅓ or 33	6	8 in wheat		0	7	0¼)		(94·955,489
⅓ or 33	6	8 in barley		0	3	11½ } is equivalent to		{ 168·421,052
⅓ or 33	6	8 in oats		0	2	9)		(242·424,242

Per Imp. Bush.

100 0 0

The above shows that the tithe charge was not a fixed money payment of £100, but only such a sum as the quantities of wheat, barley, and oats, which I have given, are equivalent to, according to the seven years to each preceding Christmas. And here I must remark that through the present defective system of making corn returns, it acts most unfairly upon the tenant-farmer and tithe-payer in general. I will give a few reasons ; and first, insufficiency of markets where the returns are furnished from, there being only 150 markets out of 798, where they are made, and few of these where inferior qualities of wheat and barley are grown. Take Wiltshire, for instance, not the richest of our counties—only one market furnishes returns in that county, no returns being made even at Salisbury or Devizes. I have gathered that at Warminster not one-fourth of the corn sold is ever returned, and this county is not alone in proving the imperfect system, for at a meeting of the Worcestershire Chamber of Agriculture recently, complaints were made that out of 40 dealers attending Worcester market, not more than four make the returns required by law. At Wakefield, Yorkshire, one of the chief markets in our country, it has been stated that for six weeks no single sale was returned. In most markets, upon inspection, no doubt, it would be found that a few of the dealers, who generally attend certain markets, make them, but that the majority of them set the law at defiance, knowing that although they are liable to a penalty of £20 for not making a true return, the law is never enforced. At the present time the ordinary tithe is about 7s. per acre, in some parishes more, excepting on woodland, where the charge is about 1s. 6d. and 2s. per acre in some parishes. There are other causes whereby the tithe-payer has been unjustly compelled by law to pay more than he should have done if the corn returns were furnished fairly. The tail and inferior corn being consumed on the farms, consequently does not come in the corn returns. Again, a great deal of corn is sold by weight, instead of by the " Imperial bushel," as the Act states in Section 57. Another evil we suffer from in consequence of the buyer instead of the grower making the return is, that corn is often sold in the first place at some distant market, and resold, perhaps more than once, by dealers, before it reaches the market selected for furnishing returns, when the price there made includes more than one profit and cost of freight. Mr. James J. Wheble, a Berkshire landowner, writing to the *Mark Lane Express* of the 17th of May last, quoted the letter of a Berkshire farmer, who points out that if averages were taken justly, the present value of £100 tithe would be £88 instead of £112.

Pressure of business during the past session of Parliament, coupled with opposition from Colonel Barne, the Conservative member for East Suffolk, who persisted in preventing it from coming on by a blocking notice, was the reason why Mr Chamberlain's promised bill to amend the taking of the corn averages did not come before the House. Upon reading the draft of this Corn Returns bill, I come to the conclusion, although it is in the right direction, as it fails to provide for basing the official averages alone on the growers' prices, and also takes no account of the tail corn which does not find its way into the markets, being unsaleable, it will be inadequate to wholly remedy the present defective system in the averages. I will, by way of illustration, endeavour to show how unfairly the septennial takings of the corn averages bear upon certain farmers. A father takes a farm for his son at Michaelmas, 1877; the corn crops for the previous seven years have been a fair average, with good prices (or at least they should have been if we are to be guided by the £100 worth of tithe in the years I am alluding to); the first year he has been in business, and the two following ones, he has poor crops, and through strong foreign competition, low prices; yet he has to pay on the previous good years he has not shared in—thus in 1878, he pays 12¾ per cent. above par, next year 11 6-8ths (one of the most disastrous years upon record), and this year 9⅞ per cent. instead of paying under £90 on the £100 worth of tithe, if returns were taken fairly. Looking from the landlords' point of view, at a largely attended anti-tithe meeting held at Wokingham on Nov. 11, 1879, Mr J. J. Wheble said, "My father bought his land subject to £50 tithes, but since the Commutation Act it had been raised to £130." Mr. George Palmer, M.P., who attended the meeting, said, "If it was a fact that the tithe in the district of Wokingham, before the Commutation Act, was £300, and now was £2,000, he thought that was sufficient grounds of itself for enquiring into the operation of the Act."

Section 81 gives power to the tithe-receiver to distrain upon crops and live or dead stock when tithes are in arrear twenty-one days. On the 21st of last May I had a notice of distraint from one of the tithe-receivers of Cudham, Kent, for tithes due April 1st. I merely mention this to show that at times the tithe-receiver resorts to this cruel power the law has placed in his hands in a very sharp way. It acts very unjustly, especially to tradesmen. For instance, a farmer fails; amongst other tradesmen he owes the wheelwright for new waggons and carts, £100; the landlord and tithe-receiver distrain upon his produce or cattle for rent and tithe; they get 20s. in the £, the wheelwright nothing. If the landlord loses his rent, he only loses the interest upon his capital, but the wheelwright loses his capital and interest as well. Section 84 is a rather amusing clause, as it relates specially to the recovery of rent charges from Quakers. I suppose it was considered at the time that members of the Society of Friends would be more adverse to the Act than other sects. There have been several large anti-tithe meetings in Kent, and at one held at Maidstone on January 14th, 1880, Mr. P. Brine, a farmer of Hawkhurst, setting forth proofs of the failure of the 1836 Act, as far as justice goes, stated that from the passing of that Act up to the present time the average of £100 worth of tithe was £103 2s. 1¼d. In several parishes where I farm a great deal of the hill land is not worth 5s. per acre, rent and tithe together, and yet there is a charge of about 7s. per acre tithe upon it;

consequently no tenant will farm it, as the landowner will not let it for less than 5s per acre, and in some instances where landlords make miserable attempts to farm it, through want of capital and judgment, the land returns but little produce as food for man. I could give numberless proofs to show that the burden of tithes are too heavy for the tenant-farmer. In the parish of Ashford, Kent, which, far from being a poor part of the country, is rather the reverse, at the time I am writing, there are no less than twenty farms, comprising 3350 acres, advertised to let. The number of sales of farming live and dead stock advertised for next month is beyond precedent, especially in the home counties. In Kent there are now 80,000 acres of woodland, and I have been told by land stewards on several estates, it pays better than the land let as farms. There is only 42 per cent. of the land that is cultivated, exclusive of permanent grass, in this county, which is called the garden of England. I will now give my opinion—

HOW TO DEAL WITH ORDINARY TITHES.

As I have endeavoured to show, tithes are a heavy burden upon the producer of food, and if something is not done soon by Parliament, they will be the means of throwing out of cultivation many acres of land, which would not only be a loss to the landowner, but an injury to the labourer ; and consequently the tradesman would suffer, and the country at large. As the Tithe Commutation Act of 1836 is so disfigured by inequalities and pregnant with injustice to the payer of tithes in my opinion, I would propose that this and all recent Acts of Parliament relating to tithes be repealed in the next Session, and a short Act passed leaving the commutation of tithes, as agreed upon in 1836, to be the same ; also, the portion and the standard price per bushel the same, viz. :—One-third in wheat, £33 6s. 8d., at 7s. 0¼d. per Imperial bushel ; one-third in barley, £33 6s. 8d., at 3s. 11½d. per Imperial bushel ; one-third in oats, £33 6s. 8d., at 2s. 9d. per Imperial bushel. All corn to be sold by the Imperial bushel only. Returns to be made by the sellers only ; penalty for not making a true return, £20. A tithe commissioner to be appointed to supply every occupier of land with forms to fill in with the price per Imperial bushel, stating buyer's name and address ; when filled in the form to be sent free by post to a department that shall be named, the taking of the averages to be triennial, 10 per cent. to be allowed off in consideration of inferior corn, which, being unfit for market, is consumed at home. This tithe to be paid by the landowner, and it to be compulsory upon him to pay it. In cases where he has tenants under leases, the tenant to pay the landowner an equivalent sum in lieu of tithes until the expiration of his or her lease. Also, that it be unlawful for the receiver of tithes to apply to any occupier for any sum for tithes after this Act comes into force. In cases of non-payment of tithes by landowners, the tithe owners can have recourse to the Law of Distress (so long as the law remains on the statute book), and distrain upon the land, and sell so much of the land as may be required to recover the amount in arrear for tithes, and in the case of a tenant occupying such lands as shall be sold, sufficient can be sold to compensate the tenant for his lease, if any, also crops, cultivations, all his unexhausted improvements ; the amount to be paid to him within two weeks after the sale.

Part II.—EXTRAORDINARY TITHE.

This tithe is nothing more nor less than a direct tax upon labour and capital, and a discouragement to certain industries. Instead of being levied on the soil according to its richness, the description of the crop grown was taken into consideration, without regard to the extra capital required and labour employed in producing it. Again, the inequalities are a great mystery, even in the present day, as will be seen in my remarks further on. Under the Tithe Commutation Act of 1836, in addition to the ordinary tithe, which is about 7s. per acre, and more in some parishes, an extraordinary tithe was levied upon hops and market-garden grounds, the latter meaning where vegetables are grown, the extra tithe not being imposed upon fruit plantations until 1839, under the Tithe Commutation Amendment Act. This extra wealth added to the clergyman's income at the expense of the fruit grower is a severe tax upon his energies; for instance, take Eynsford parish, in Kent; area, 3536 acres, with a great deal of heavy hill land now going out of cultivation, three farms, averaging 250 acres each, being tenantless on one estate, and not touched by the landowner. At the time of the Commutation Act, 1836, the tithes were commuted at £1080 in this parish, being—Rectorial, £600; Vicarial, £480. Under the Tithe Commutation Amendment Act, 1839, an impost of 7s. per acre was put upon the fruit plantations, most of them being previously woodland. There are about 1000 acres of fruit plantations in the parish; rateable value of the whole parish in 1871, £6233; population, 1433, with very little increase in either up to the present time. There is no extraordinary tithe on fruit in the adjoining parish of Shoreham. I can refer my readers to Section 42 of the 1836 Act, which I have given previously, but not commented upon. It will be seen that this section refers only to certain districts where this extraordinary tithe could be imposed upon hops and market-garden grounds; but under a subsequent Act, 23 and 24 Vic., c. 93, sec. 42 (1860), any parish is liable to this extra tithe if steps are taken to make the parish chargeable as required by the Act. The extra charges upon hop grounds vary so much that it is no little puzzle to understand how the valuers and tithe commissioners arrived at the amounts, in many parishes the fertility of the soil being equal, while there is vast difference in the charge. In Kent there are about 43,400 acres of hops charged with this tithe, and I should not be exaggerating if I said it would average 15s. per acre, as this would be rather under the average. I will give a few parishes, the charges of which I have taken from farmers who have actually paid these amounts at per acre : Sevenoaks, 18s. ; Shoreham, 14s. ; Eynsford, 12s. ; Halstead, 10s. ; Wrotham, £1 ; Westerham, 18s. ; Edenbridge, 18s. ; Chiddingstone, 12s. ; Brasted, 15s. 4½d. ; Thurnham, 10s. ; Seal, 16s. ; Yalding, 18s. ; Hollinbourne, 10s. ; Ulcomb, 16s. 6d. ; Chart Sutton, 15s. ; Sutton Valence, 13s. to 18s. ; Cooling, 4s. ; Higham, 12s. ; Sittingbourne, 12s. ; Tonbridge, 18s. ; Hartlip, 8s. ; Minster, 10s. ; Otham, 18s. ; Gillingham, near Chatham, 7s. ; Boughton Malherbe, 18s. ; Boughton Mouchelsea, 15s. ; Leeds, 14s. ; Headcorn, 16s. ; East Sutton, 18s. ; Cliffe at Hoo, 10s. ; Faversham, 10s. ; Marden, 16s. ; Ash, 12s. ; Bearstead, near Maidstone, 18s. ; Kemsing, 4s. ; Canterbury, 12s. ; Doddington, 10s. ; Hayes, 10s. ; Goodnestone, next Faversham, 10s. There are a few parishes in this country where this extra charge is not imposed. I will name two, Cranbrook and Benenden.

The extra charge commences the first year of polling the hops, when half is charged. The following year, when they are in full poll the whole amount is charged. When the hops are grubbed, and the garden used for corn, &c. (six months' notice being given to the clergyman of the alteration), the extra tithe ceases. Also in the case of fruit plantation and market garden grounds it ceases in like manner.

The corn averages also bear upon this tithe ; for instance, any one having £100 of extraordinary tithe to pay, as the average stood last year, would have to pay £111 15s. 1½d. This refers to market gardens and fruit plantations as well as hop grounds. In Sussex there are about 9900 acres of hop gardens charged with this extra tithe. By what I have ascertained from farmers in that county, I find the lowest is 14s. per acre, and highest 19s., excepting in Ifield which is 8s. per acre. I will give a few parishes: Brede 18s. per acre, Beckley 17s., Peasmarsh 18s., Westfield 18s.; Burwash 14s., Ticehurst 17s., Etchingham 17s. I could find no parish where this extra tithe upon hops did not exist in this county.

In Surrey, there are about 2300 acres of hops on which extraordinary tithe is charged, varying from 12s. to £1 10s. per acre. Although hops are grown in Tandridge and Crowhurst parishes of this county, no extraordinary tithe is charged. Upon visiting Farnham, on August 5th, I found that the extraordinary tithe upon hops was ranged in six classes, from 13s. 4d. to £1 10s. per acre, whereas in Limpsfield and Oxted parishes, in the south-east of the county, it is 16s. 9d. In Hampshire about 3000 acres of hops are charged with extraordinary tithe, varying from 12s. to £1 per acre. On visiting Alton, in that county, I found that in the parish of Neatham no extraordinary tithe was charged upon the hops. At Alton, the extraordinary tithe on hops is £1 per acre; Binsted, £1; Holybourne, 13s. 4d.; Kingsley, 13s. 4d.; East Worldham, £1; West Worldham, 12s.; Hartley, 15s.; Selbourne, 13s. 4d.; Bentley, £1; East Tisted, 13s. 4d. In Herefordshire there are about 5900 acres of hops chargeable with extraordinary tithe, grown in sixteen parishes. On visiting Hereford, on August 18th, I ascertained from hop growers that the extraordinary tithe on hop yards (as they are termed there) would average 6s. per acre, excepting in the parishes of Bosbury and Mortiford, where there is none. In Worcestershire, 2609 acres of hops are charged with extraordinary tithe, and I found upon visiting Worcester, August 21st, that it averaged from 5s. to 10s. per acre.

The extraordinary tithe upon fruit plantations and

market garden grounds varies from 4s. to 18s. per acre, the most common charge being about 7s. or 8s. per acre. Half of the extra charge is imposed upon fruit grounds (bushtrees) upon the second year from the commencement of the fresh planting, and the full charge on the third year. As there are many parishes in England where this extra charge is not imposed, although it could be by following out what is required by the Tithe Act of 1860, I have no means at hand whereby I can ascertain the actual acreage so charged. I will merely give the number of acres from the Agricultural returns by the Board of Trade :—Orchards in Great Britain, 180,000 acres ; market gardens, 41,000 acres. I will state the amounts of the extra charge upon fruit grounds in a few parishes ; Eynsford, 7s per acre ; next parish of Shoreham, none ; Farnborough, 7s ; Sutton-at-Hone, 9s ; next parish of Horton Kirby, none ; Farningham, 8s. ; St. Mary Cray, 8s. ; Cobham, near Gravesend, 8s.; Orpington, 8s. ; Erith, 10s. ; Gillingham, 7s. ; Hoo, 12s. ; Cooling, 4s. ; East Sutton, 18s. ; Sutton Valence, 18s. ; Leeds, 18s. ; Canterbury none ; Boughton Malherbe, 18s. ; Cranbrook, none ; Bexley none ; Westerham, 18s. ; Edenbridge, 18s. ; Chart Sutton, 8s. 6d. These are parishes in the county of Kent, and charged under the Tithe Commutation Act of 1839. I will now give a few parishes where the extra charge has been made under the 1860 Act, and date of the award when confirmed—fruit or market garden grounds. Plumstead, Kent, 6s. per acre, September 5, 1871 ; Offenham, Worcestershire, 4s., August 14, 1863 ; Lancing, Sussex, 6s., September 27, 1866 ; Henfield, Sussex, 4s. 6d., July 18, 1867 ; Edburton, Sussex, 4s., October 8, 1868 ; Thakeham, Sussex, 3s. 6d., February 8, 1872.

In Surrey, under the 1839 Act, Limpsfield was charged 16s. 9d. per acre, and Oxted, 16s. 9d. Isleworth, in Middlesex, 7s. I may here mention that although woodland, at the time of the Commutation Act, 1836, was charged about 2s.

per acre, as ordinary tithe, and in some parishes less, if it is grubbed up and planted with hops, or fruit, the existing extraordinary tithe in that parish is imposed upon this newly planted ground. For instance, take Eynsford parish, in Kent, which only pays 1s. 6d. per acre upon woodland which is greatly to the advantage of the landowners who held almost all their woodland at the time of the passing of the 1836 Act, or it is a question if even it would have been commuted so low. When grubbed up at the expense of fruit growers or farmers, and brought into cultivation, extra charges of 7s. on fruit, and 12s. per acre on hop grounds are imposed. I will here mention that according to the agricultural returns just issued from the Board of Trade, during the last eight years there has been nearly 10 per cent. increase of newly-planted woods. In 1872 there were 2,187,000 acres, and in 1880, 2,409,000. I will now give three Sections of the Tithe Commutation Amendment Act, dated 17th August, 1839 :—

CAP. 42.—An Act to explain and amend the Acts for the Commutation of Tithes in England and Wales, was passed.

26. And be it enacted, That in case any of the lands in a parish the tithes whereof shall be in course of commutation under the provisions of the said first recited Act shall be orchards or fruit plantations, and notice in writing, under the hands of any of the owners thereof whose interest therein shall not be less than two thirds of the whole of the orchards and fruit plantations in such parish, shall be given to the valuers or commissioners or assistant commissioner by whom any apportionment provided for by the said Act shall be made at any time before the draught of such apportionment shall be framed that the Tithes thereof should be distinguished into two parts, the amount which shall be charged by any such apportionment upon the several orchards and fruit plantations in such parish shall be distinguished into two parts accordingly, and the same shall be called the Ordinary Charge and the Extraordinary Fruit Charge ; and the Extraordinary Charge shall be a rate per imperial acre,

and so in proportion for less quantities of ground, according to the discretion of the valuers or commissioners or assistant commissioner by whom such apportionment shall be made as aforesaid.

27. And be it enacted, That all lands the Tithes whereof shall have been commuted under the said Act, which shall be situate within the limits of any parish in which an Extraordinary Fruit Charge shall have been distinguished as aforesaid at time of commutation, and which shall be newly cultivated as orchard or fruit plantations at any time after such commutation, shall be charged with an additional amount of rent-charge per imperial acre equal to the extraordinary Fruit Charge per acre in that parish : Provided always, that no such additional amount shall be charged in respect of any plantation of apples, pears, plums, cherries, and filberts, or of any one or more of those fruits, during the first five years, and half only of such additional amount during each of the next succeeding five years of such new cultivation thereof ; and that no such additional amount shall be charged in respect of any plantation of gooseberries, currants, or raspberries, or of any one or more of those fruits, during the first two years, and half only of such additional amount during each of the next succeeding two years of such new cultivation thereof ; and that no such additional amount shall be charged in respect of any mixed plantation of apples, pears, plums, cherries, or filberts, and of gooseberries, currants, or raspberries during the first three years, and half only of such additional amount during each of the next succeeding three years, of such new cultivation thereof.

32. And be it enacted, that for the purpose of fixing any charge for the Tithes of hops or fruit, or any mixed plantation as aforesaid, the Commissioners may, if they see fit, assign the parish or lands in respect of which due notice shall have been given, requiring the Tithes thereof to be separately valued, as required by the said first recited Act, or any part or parts of such parish or lands, as a district under the provisions of the said Act, and may fix a charge upon such lands in respect of the Tithes of hops or fruit as the rent-charge to prevail and to be established in respect of the same, without specific reference in the award to any other parish or lands, but having regard nevertheless to the general amount

of compositions which they shall find to have prevailed in other parishes of a similar description, and not to the money payments in the parish under consideration, or the value of the Tithes in kind therein.

In Section 26 it will be seen that the power, as usual, rests with the large landowner to charge this impost on fruit ground.

Section 27 provides that newly-cultivated fruit plantations be charged an additional sum.

Section 28, which I do not give, relieves fruit plantations, when displanted, from the additional charge.

The next Act, of which I will give three clauses, is dated 13th August, 1860, 23 and 24 Vic., c. 93. " An Act to amend and further extend the Acts for the Commutation of Tithes in England and Wales."

Section 42 gives further power to the Commissioners to levy extraordinary tithes in parishes or districts where none existed previously. I will just give a little of my own experience with respect to this clause. In 1865 I took a lease of a farm at Halstead, Kent, for 14 years, and planted several acres of hops in that parish, knowing there were no extraordinary tithes upon them, there being only two roods at the time of the Commutation Act, 1836. The salary of the clergyman was arrived at from the ordinary tithe, but on the 10th of September, 1867, a Vestry was called, a Tithe Commissioner attended, and although every tenant at the meeting (which was crowded) raised his voice at the fresh impost, because one landowner and the clergyman consented, 10s. per acre was charged. I quote this to show the danger we are under so long as the various Tithe Acts remain un-repealed :—

42. Whenever the Commissioners are requested in the manner provided by the said recited Acts to charge an additional rent-charge by way of extraordinary charge upon

any hop grounds or market gardens newly cultivated as such beyond the limits of any district for which an extraordinary charge for hop grounds or market gardens respectively shall have been already distinguished, the Commissioners may declare the lands in the parish in which such newly cultivated hop grounds or market gardens are situate a district within which the extraordinary charge to be then fixed by them shall be thereafter payable.

43. For the purpose of ascertaining the extent of the land cultivated as hop grounds or market gardens, the person to whom any extraordinary charge upon such land is or would be payable, his agents or servants, at all reasonable times, may enter upon the said land, and make an admeasurement and plan of the same, without being subject to any action or molestation for so doing.

44. This Act shall be taken and construed as part of the said first-recited Act. as amended and extended by the several Acts passed for the amendment thereof, and by this Act.

Of all the tithes, the extraordinary one is the most obnoxious, and is therefore disliked by all farmers, especially in Kent, more being paid in that county than any other; hence the agitations and meetings for its abolition. On June the 3rd, a deputation of farmers waited upon the President of the Board of Trade, urging its abolition. On the 23rd of June a large and influential meeting w s held at Swanley, near Farningham, Kent, and another was held at Maidstone, on the 8th of July. From these meetings emanated petitions to Parliament which have been freely signed in Kent and Sussex, for the abolition in an equitable manner of the Extraordinary Tithe, and as those petitions refer to an Act of 1873, which being a short one, I give it in its entirety, as it may be of use to any who are without it :—

[36 and 37 Vict.] Tithe Commutation Acts Amendment.

[Cн. 42.]—" An Act for amending the Tithe Commutation Acts with respect to Market Gardens." [21st July, 1873.]

Whereas by the Tithe Commutation Acts (described in the schedule to this Act) provision is made for the commutation into a permanent rent-charge of the tithes leviable in the several parishes in England and Wales :

And whereas it is expedient to amend the said Acts in respect of the sections of such Acts in the said schedule particularly mentioned :—

Be it therefore enacted by the Queen's most Excellent Majesty, by and with the advice and consent of the Lords Spiritual and Temporal, and Commons, in this present Parliament assembled, and by the authority of the same, as follows :

1. So much of such sections, and of the powers therein contained conferred on the Tithe Commissioners, as provide for the charging of an additional rent-charge by way of extraordinary charge on market gardens newly cultivated as such, shall extend and apply only to a parish in which an extraordinary charge for market gardens was distinguished at the time of commutation.

2. Nothing in this Act shall affect or be deemed to apply to any proceedings taken or to be taken in relation to the charging of an additional rent-charge by way of extraordinary charge on market-gardens newly cultivated as such in any case where an award in that behalf was made and confirmed, or where an application was made to the Tithe Commissioners to charge an additional rent-charge by way of extraordinary charge upon any market gardens newly cultivated as such, before the commencement of the present session of Parliament.

3. This Act shall be construed and have effect as one Act with the Tithe Commutation Acts, and may be cited as " The Tithe Commutation Acts Amendment Act, 1873."

I will just make a few remarks as to how this Act was brought about, and what benefit it is to some market gardeners. At that time through an attempt by tithe-receivers in Cornwall to impose an extraordinary tithe of 30s. per acre, on new ground reclaimed by the industry of Cornish men, and used as market gardens by them, through agitating in the matter, an application was made to Parliament to protect that industry from this unjust impost. The Bill was referred to a select committee, and this Act was passed, which on perusal will be seen, provides that in no future case should this extra tax be charged upon market gardens (not fruit plantations, which are distinct from them), unless the parish in which they were situated had been at the time of the commutation of the tithes distinguished as a parish liable to the extraordinary tithe. Therefore it will be seen that there are now some parishes where this extra tax is levied, while others are free from it. When the Bill was before Parliament it applied to hop plantations as well as market garden grounds, but some of the Kentish members who were supposed to represent hop growers in that county, said that the farmers were not anxious to be relieved from the extraordinary tithe on hops, which proves in some measure that we want men from our own ranks, independent of party, to truly represent our interests.

It will thus be evident that by the passing of this Act a certain amount of good was gained, or rather further imposition stopped, by market gardeners in Cornwall ventilating their grievance before the public ; and I am glad to see that the agitation now going on in the hop and fruit growing counties, and the many letters in country papers, and some in the London press, have at least brought one member of Parliament to come to our assistance ; I am referring to Mr. F. A. Inderwick, Q.C., the Liberal member for Rye, Sussex, who gave notice on the 4th of September :—"Early next Session to bring in a Bill to encourage the cultivation of hops, fruit, and market garden produce, by amending the laws relating to the imposition of extraordinary tithes." As I have not at present seen the draft of this Bill, I cannot make any comment upon it ; but of one thing I am certain, that he will gain the thanks of all agriculturists, especially of those who are directly interested in that particular industry, by seeking to relieve them from this heavy and unjust impost. Mr. Inderwick has already presented seventeen petitions to Parliament, " praying that some equitable plan should be devised whereby the whole of the extraordinary tithes shall be abolished, &c.," signed by hop and fruit growers, from Kent and Sussex ; also Mr. James Howard, Liberal member for Bedford, and Sir E. Filmer, Conservative member for Mid-Kent, and the two Conservative members for East Sussex, have presented eighteen similar petitions, containing in all 797 signatures. Next Session there will be many more presented to Parliament from Kent, Sussex, Surrey, Hereford, Worcester, and Hampshire, there being petitions in course of signature in parishes of these counties where hops, fruit, or market garden produce are cultivated. I will now suggest to my readers my idea

HOW TO DEAL WITH EXTRAORDINARY TITHES.

A short Act of Parliament, to be called the " Extraordinary Tithes Compulsory Redemption Act," should be passed, declaring that at a certain period, all extraordinary tithes shall be redeemed, landowners in a reasonable time to pay the receivers of these tithes (who are with few exceptions clergymen of the Church of England), life and vested interest, it to be compulsory upon receivers of tithes to sell, Government to grant loans to the landowners where required, upon easy terms, for the purpose of redeeming the said tithes. After the passing of this Act any agreement or lease binding the tenant to pay the landowner an extra sum per year in " consideration " of being relieved of these tithes will be useless, and of no effect in courts of justice.

CONCLUSION.

I hope no one will consider me unfair in arguing that the ordinary tithes shall henceforth be paid by the landowner, for I consider he is the only person who should pay this impost. It has been argued over and over again that it is a landowners' question, a tax upon his land. Granted!

Then I say by all means let him pay his own taxes, and not endeavour to throw his burdens upon the poor tenant, who is breaking down every day under his load, which is too heavy for him to bear. Again, I am only asking what is done by every landowner in Scotland, in some of the Northern and Midland counties, and by a landlord in one parish where 1 farm, also by others in parts of Kent well known to me. Then, as to the alteration of taking the corn averages which I propose. It is merely to endeavour to get a correct return. In Scotland they already manage this far more satisfactorily than we do, the farmers meeting an officer and others appointed for the purpose every spring, and giving the results of their sales of corn. I am well aware that an alteration is needed in the price of wheat, and that the quantity should be lessened in wheat for the averages; but my object is to first give this a fair trial for at least three years, and then, if necessary, further legislation can be effected to improve upon it. Why I suggest that the Act should be compulsory in making the landowner pay the ordinary tithe is, that I am certain that any other legislation would be useless. I say this with all due respect to landowners and with a considerable amount of reluctance. Take for instance the Agricultural Holdings Act, with its permissive clause; why, it is a dead-letter, it is worthless!

Again, if the tenant has to insist upon securing any benefit from any Act of Parliament, from his landlord, instead of that Act compelling the stronger person, the land-owner, to carry it out, it becomes useless to the tenant; he being the weaker of the two, always fails in the attempt. For instance, what advantage has the farmer in the Midland and Southern counties derived from the 60th section of the Act, 6 and 7 William IV., cap. 71, passed in 1836, which pro-vides that any tenant paying the tithe shall be entitled to deduct the amount thereof from the rent payable by him to his landlord? But notice—he must insist upon the observance of this from his landlord when taking his farm. On the other hand, how few landowners have sought to obtain the redemption of tithes under the Act of 1878 (see 41 and 42 Vic., cap. 42, section 4). Such redemption on reasonable terms would improve the value of their estates, and would relieve the tenant from all concern with the tithe ; but as there is nothing compulsory in the Act, its good intentions are lost.

The question might arise. How will this alteration, if made law, affect the tenant-farmer and landowner? The tenant, of course, will have to pay more rent, but not so much as he now does, rent and tithes together ; consequently his rates and taxes would be reduced, as the tithe charge is assessed to the income taxes and poor rates, which is a fresh burthen since 1836, and he will be relieved from paying a tax so obnoxious to him. On the other hand, the landowner, although after paying tithes and striking a balance from rent he receives, may find it less for a time—yet, in the long run, he will prove he is no loser by the change. Instead of his farms being tenantless, they will be occupied, and he will not have to resort to the system of allowing 10 to 25 per cent. deduction off his rents. The cultivation of fruit, market gardens, and hop grounds, being freed from the extraordinary tithe will increase in acreage, and stop to a considerable extent the great increase of imports of hops, fruit, and vegetables, that should be grown at home, thus keeping the extra labour required to produce them, as well as the money, at home. And looking at a landowner's point of view, the land thus being relieved from this extraordinary tithe, would realise more when sold than if the impost remained on. At the time when the duty was taken off hops, the extraordinary tithe upon hop plantations should have been redeemed. For instance, look at the unfair position it left us in, the duty on our hops was £1 per cwt., but on foreign hops over £4, really a prohibitory rate, and yet we still hugged the extra tax, forgetting that what land can bear in the time of protection is far different from what it can when free trade takes its place. Although this change of the person paying the tithes, who it was intended by the 1836 Act should pay them, would relieve the tenant-farmer of his greatest burden, let it not be thought that that alone will emancipate him from the present distressful condition that he has by degrees drifted into, but as I am dealing with tithes, I will not dwell upon the other burdens which press heavily upon him, but merely mention some of the foremost which most directly affect him, and with reference to which the Committee of the Farmers' Alliance on the 17th of September, in London, passed a resolution to the effect that they required the immediate attention of Government, viz., " To stimulate the improved cultivation of the land, especially by obtaining security for the capital of tenants invested in the improvement of their holdings ; to obtain the abolition of class privileges involved in the Law of Distress ; to secure to ratepayers their legitimate share of County Government ; to obtain a fair apportionment of local burdens between landlord and tenant." I firmly believe when the farmer is relieved of the tithes, and the above reforms advocated by the Farmers' Alliance are accomplished, he will be in a position to grow corn at such a cost as will enable him to compete with the foreigner, and the representatives of the people will be able to congratulate themselves on having done their duty. The land question is not only a landowners' and farmers', but a national one, and no country can prosper long where agriculture is upon the decline. I am certainly reiterating the words of farmers in saying we want no favours, no class legislation, but

We ask for justice, this we will demand,
Just laws under which to till our Nation's land.

www.ingramcontent.com/pod-product-compliance
Lightning Source LLC
Chambersburg PA
CBHW032134080426
42733CB00008B/1075

* 9 7 8 3 3 3 7 0 3 7 2 1 5 *